PLAINS BOUND:
FRAGILE CARGO

Revealing Orphan Train Reality

WRITTEN BY: CHARLOTTE M. ENDORF
ILLUSTRATED BY: SARAH M. ENDORF

Outskirts Press, Inc.
Denver, Colorado

Plains Bound: Fragile Cargo
Revealing Orphan Train Reality
All Rights Reserved
Copyright © 2005 Charlotte M. Endorf

Outskirts Press
http://www.outskirtspress.com

ISBN-10: 1-59800-235-X
ISBN-13: 978-1-59800-235-5

Library of Congress Control Number: 2005937453

Outskirts Press and the "OP" logo are trademarks belonging to
Outskirts Press, Inc.

Printed in the United States of America

PRAISE FOR *PLAINS BOUND: FRAGILE CARGO*

"Wow, the time and effort spent capturing a piece of history will chronicle a part of history that would have otherwise been lost. *Plains Bound: Fragile Cargo* includes fascinating stories of which I would never have been aware. Sincere thanks for sharing and all of the effort you put into capturing this part of history. *Plains Bound: Fragile Cargo* is a must-read for anyone who likes history. Lester's poem said it best,

> 'But when you know their story
> Your troubles seem to pale.'

His wisdom is inspiring! Great work! I wish Charlotte Endorf much success in her speaking career. I hope many people will be blessed by hearing her tell the stories of the Orphan Train."

~Darren LaCroix
Author, Comedian, 2001 World
Champion of Public Speaking

"Charlotte Endorf has captured the essence of the powerful 'can do' spirit of Orphan Train riders—true survivors in every sense of the word. Endorf allows this trait to shine through the telling of stories by individual riders or by their descendants. She has truly presented this little-known era in America's history in a moving and informative way. Her many hours of research documenting the lives of so many riders shall not be spent in vain. Readers for years to come will enjoy and learn from her work. I'm grateful to Charlotte Endorf for preserving the history of the Orphan Train Riders in a caring manner as so many others involved with the Orphan Train Heritage Society of America have done since 1986."

~Mary Ellen Johnson
Founder of the Orphan Train Heritage
Society of America, Inc.

"Charlotte and Sarah have successfully prepared a heart-warming account of an important part of American History which needs to be told and remembered. The New York City children who rode the rails to a new life were placed across America and greatly impacted the development of our country. This book is an opportunity to get to know a few of the children and learn what became of them. I recommend this book for all ages and encourage schools to add it to their curriculum. If you want to learn more, visit the Madison County Museum in Madison, Nebraska, where you can see the permanent display of Orphan Train Rider memorabilia."

~Carol Robertson
Executive Director of the Madison County
Historical Society and Former Educator

"*Plains Bound: Fragile Cargo* describes an important part of our nation's history that could soon be forgotten as Orphan Train riders age and pass on. I am glad that Charlotte took the time to travel over 3,000 miles to interview these 'gems' that shared such a human part of our U.S. and Nebraska history! I didn't know much about the Orphan Train before, but I plan to read more so that I can share this remarkable part of history with my 4th grade students. Thank you, Charlotte!"

~Diane Scott
Elementary School Teacher

"Many people have some understanding of the Orphan Trains, but most do not really know the history. Charlotte Endorf has illuminated the lives of those who experienced the Orphan Trains firsthand, and were left at the many stations across the Great Plains. The Orphan Train children became woven into the fabric of Great Plains society and the region's communities. Endorf has allowed them to tell their stories. Positive and negative experiences are revealed."

~Raymond D. Screws, Ph.D.
Senior Program Officer
Nebraska Humanities Council

"*Plains Bound* is a resonant account of the Orphan Train and some of our nation's most rapidly disappearing heroes.

The book is an immensely readable examination of the Nebraska Orphan Train experience as told by those who, by fate, were cast as players in this real life historical drama. Author Endorf finds herself both humbled and in awe of the fragile humanity she encountered—survivors who were victorious over misfortunes that would have crushed the less determined and doomed the ones without hope."

~Susan Sutton
President of the National Orphan Train
Complex; Humanities Dean,
Cloud County Community College

"*Plains Bound: Fragile Cargo* is a wonderful compilation of Orphan Train riders' stories from Nebraska. Endorf presents an accurate and fair representation of what some of the children experienced through their own words. It is a good introduction for those seeking a glimpse into the world of an Orphan Train rider."

~Stephanie Haiar
Curator of the National Orphan Train
Complex

"I have always thought my Mother, my Auntie Lois, and my Auntie Rene (Irene) were extraordinary women. The personal histories of these brave and lonely children are rich, compelling, and full of dramatic twists and turns that will tug at the readers' heartstrings. In preserving their story, along with those of other courageous riders, Ms. Endorf has ensured that the historical impact of their lives will not be forgotten."

~Anita Ertle
Daughter of Merle (Chapter 10)
College Librarian

YOUTH PRAISE FOR
PLAINS BOUND: FRAGILE CARGO

I have been told all ages will love *Plains Bound: Fragile Cargo.* I surveyed a range of children from $2^{nd} - 7^{th}$ grade just to see their viewpoint on the book. I asked each child the same set of questions. Some of the children responded with mere answers while others shared complete paragraphs for printing:

- Have you ever studied Orphan Trains in school or did you know anything about Orphan Trains before reading this? **No, I didn't.**
- What do you think of the cover? **Awesome!** Is it bright enough to draw kids attention? **Definitely!** Do you pick up books by the cover? **Sometimes.**
- The Orphan Train history is now a part of many school history books. Is this a topic you'd like to learn more about by having a speaker come into your school with a fun assembly? **Sure, why not?**
- Is this a book that you think would be popular in your school library? **Definitely!** Would you recommend this book to other kids your age? **Of Course!**
- What do you think of the illustrations? **Awesome!**

~Patrick Meuret
11 years old
5th grade

- Have you ever studied Orphan Trains in school or did you know anything about Orphan Trains before reading this? **Yes, I have studied Orphan Trains in school. I learned a lot about them in reading class.**
- What do you think of the cover? **The cover of the book is awesome. It definitely draws my attention!** What do you think of the illustrations? **I like all of the pictures. I wish I could draw that good!**
- The Orphan Train history is now a part of many school history books. Is this a topic you'd like to learn more about by having a

speaker come into your school with a fun assembly? Yes, definitely!

- Is this a book that you think would be popular in your school library? I really enjoyed reading it! I think that the kids in my school would also love the book! Would you recommend this book to other kids your age? Yes, I recommend *Plains Bound: Fragile Cargo* to other kids my age!

~Conner Pahl
11 years old
6th grade

- Have you ever studied Orphan Trains in school or did you know anything about Orphan Trains before reading this? No, we haven't gotten there yet!
- What do you think of the cover? I like the cover of the book. It is just right!
- Is this a topic you'd like to learn more about by having a speaker come into your school with a fun assembly? Yes! We write a report about Nebraska in 4th grade, so this fits right in!
- Is this a book that you think would be popular in your school library? Yes! Would you recommend this book to other kids your age? Yes, I think my class would love it!
- What do you think of the illustrations? I really like the train! Sarah is so talented!

~Jessa Siebe
9 ½ years old
4th Grade

- Have you ever studied Orphan Trains in school or did you know anything about Orphan Trains before reading this? No, I have never studied the Orphan Trains before reading this book.
- Do you sometimes pick up a book by its cover? Yes, I sometimes pick up a book by the cover. The clouds on the cover drew me in!

- Is this a topic you'd like to learn more about by having a speaker come into your school with a fun assembly? Yes! I think it would be really cool to have someone come to my school so I could learn more about Orphan Trains!
- Would you recommend this book to other kids your age? The book was a little hard for me to read as a 2nd grader but my Dad helped me!
- What do you think of the illustrations? I really liked the illustrations!

~Madison Vetch
8 years old
2nd Grade

"I have studied Orphan Trains in school. I have read books in my class. I think the cover is cool. With the railroad track and the sky, it is really beautiful. I think that it is bright and kids would enjoy reading it and learning about the Orphan Trains. I sometimes pick up a book by the cover or by illustrations, but most of the time I read a book because it is interesting. Yes, I think people would like it if a speaker came to our school and talked about Orphan Trains. That would be cool, because I think a lot of people would enjoy listening and learning about it. Yes, I think this book would be very popular at my school library. I think that kids would read it, and I would definitely recommend it to other kids my age and people of all ages."

~Hannah Kostal
13 years old
7th grade

"Yes, I read a book about Orphan Trains this year in 5th grade in Reading. I like the cover. The train track is cool. Yes, the colors would make you want to pick up the book and read it. Sometimes I pick up books by the cover because it looks good. Sometimes the illustrations make me read it. Yes, an assembly would be really interesting. Yes, I think a lot of kids would read *Plains Bound: Fragile Cargo* and learn more about history. Yes, I would recommend it to other kids my age and older people to read and learn about the Orphan Train."

~Steven Kostal
11 years old
5th grade

DEDICATION

For all who seek to learn about Orphan Trains. May this book touch your heart as you learn about a very remarkable and inspirational part of our American History.

In loving memory of my dear friends, Howard and Fred. Deceased Howard's website linked me to his brother Fred. Both were Orphan Train riders. Before he passed away, Fred encouraged me as a professional speaker to replace him as an active voice in taking the Orphan Train story to school children, civic organizations, museums, nursing homes, and YMCAs.

CONTENTS

Harry
His mother passed away when he was born; his father just couldn't take care of all three children so sought the Orphan Train for help.

Mary Ellen
She rode the Orphan Train to Nebraska and was later moved back to Hornell, New York, where she was adopted by another family.

The sons of Theodore Roosevelt and Mr. Hilborne L. Roosevelt maintained an active interest in the work of the Children's Aid Society Lodging House, furnishing bountiful dinners at the holidays, shirts and shoes at Christmas, and prizes for attendance and progress at night school!

His foster mother kept a wonderful diary and photo album that he has kindly shared! The words to the popular holiday song "Jolly Old St. Nicholas" were written by none other than his foster father!

Lawrence
His second placement in Nebraska landed him with his brother Lester, and allowed the boys to grow up together after all!

Marie
Her mom and dad separated when she was only age two. She and her sister and brothers were given to the orphanage.

Elsie
She wasn't allowed to ride the Orphan Train with her sister and brothers because she was hearing impaired!

Catherine (Lila)
Her name was changed from Catherine to Lila when she moved to Nebraska.

He wanted to make his parents proud and became a priest!

Robert

> *Robert learned as a little boy at the tender age of about seven that "Everybody needs somebody."*

ACKNOWLEDGEMENTS

For my husband, Kevin Endorf; my children, Sarah and Spencer Endorf; and my parents, LeRoy and Donna Vetch. Thanks for all your love, support, and encouragement!

For Brian Henderson and Jennifer Thompson, such great friends. Thanks so much for your technical assistance with this book.

For Dorothy Fletcher, another great friend, who has now helped review two books! Thanks for another three solid months of your time. Your many words and notes of support and encouragement are truly both motivational and encouraging.

For Mary Ellen Johnson, Founder of the Orphan Train Heritage Society of America, Inc. I feel very fortunate to have had the opportunity to work with you on this project. Thanks so much for sharing your expertise for the sake of helping me make this a "true-to-history" project.

For all the Orphan Train riders and their descendants who so openly shared their heartwarming stories and photos in order for me to complete this project. Your patience allowed me to gain understanding and accuracy and was greatly appreciated! You've all become such very dear friends during this short time.

To all of my other friends and relatives who provided words of encouragement along the 3,000-mile information gathering trail. Thankfully, for me, there are too many of you to mention, because I would hate to leave anybody out, but you know who you are! You're the best!

Mostly, I thank you for taking the time to read this book to learn more about this very important part of American History!

And thank you, God, for granting me the privilege of doing this work, and for allowing me the opportunity to meet and interview the many wonderful Orphan Train riders and descendants who were so willing to share their story with me so that this part of American History could be more easily understood for generations to come!

PREFACE

Great ideas begin with a dream. Americans over the years have had many big dreams. Today we enjoy the tremendous accomplishments of these brave risktakers.

To jog your memory of what occurred during this time frame and after, please enjoy these historical facts:

1903   The Wright brothers made the first successful airplane flight.

1913   Henry Ford revolutionized the business world by installing the first moving assembly line.

1920   The BAND-AID bandage was introduced.

1937   The first automatic washing machine was introduced.

1946   The first electronic computer was unveiled.

1953   The FCC approved the first color broadcast of a television show.

1969   The Internet was created to help scientists across the U.S. share research.

1975   The first commercial VCR appeared on the market.

1983   The cellular phone was introduced.

1992   The World Wide Web was introduced allowing information to be shared throughout the world.

In 2004, I could see that a very valuable part of American History would soon be lost. After a 3,000-mile trek of live interviews, featuring both Orphan Train riders and their descendants, I share with you their heartwarming and touching true stories. I, again, thank them from the bottom of my heart for being so candid about this very important period of time so that you could learn the truth instead of seeing things through rose-colored glasses.

I did a survey with adults and children over a two-year time span to see if this project was truly worthy of my time. Seeing their blank stares and listening to their varied answers on this subject convinced me that I was headed in the right direction. I decided it was important to get the stories told as soon as possible, because many of these Orphan Train riders and their descendants are over age 85 and are anxious to see the book in print.

Some of those I have interviewed have asked that I use only first names to protect their identities. I feel compelled to honor these requests for privacy. As you will note, throughout the book I have retained their first names, but have dropped their last names.

For some, once their stories have been told, closure can be put to this part of their lives. For others, this book will serve as a documented record for generations to come. This will not only keep the history alive; it will also fulfill the dreams of those who yearn to have a permanent account of their lives.

INTRODUCTION

In the 1850's there were an estimated 30,000 homeless children in New York City. These children ranged in age from infants to age 18 or so. They shared a grim common existence. Homeless and neglected, they lived in the streets and slums with no hope of a successful future. One man with tremendous dreams, Charles Loring Brace, a young minister, saw the dire needs and felt such a strong desire to help that he turned from a "well-to-do" secure lifestyle to that of a poorly-paid social worker. He founded the Children's Aid Society in 1853 and became the Society's first secretary.

Brace believed he could change the future for these children. By removing the kids from the streets and placing them in morally upright rural families in which they were needed, he thought they would have a chance of escaping a lifetime of suffering.

By the late 1860's, hundreds of babies were found on garbage heaps daily, and young children were left to fend for themselves on New York City streets. Catherine Fitzgibbons (Sister Mary Irene) of the Sisters of Charity saw the results of a poor immigrant population and a high death rate of women during childbirth. Unwed mothers were often homeless themselves, and Sister Irene's heart went out to these children.

She shared Brace's vision and enthusiasm. In 1872, with only five dollars, she started the New York-based Foundling Hospital. Like Brace, she could not have foreseen the far-reaching results of her charitable work.

The goal was to find comfortable homes with boundless advantages and opportunities. Perhaps for most children, this was achieved; however, in my interviews, I found that all were not so fortunate.

Although some Sisters of Charity orphans were infants too young to recall the journey or simply couldn't remember the ride of so many years ago, many could still remember their tag number and the wait for their predetermined parents.

Funding came from private donations, churches, and charitable organizations. This paid for clothes, food, and transportation for the children as well as salaries for the agents who accompanied them West.

The kids were scrubbed, dressed in new clothes, and put in train cars headed West. No disabled or sick kids were allowed! Almost all were white and Christian, as these were thought most likely to find homes in the West.

The trip was hard for the kids who were leaving their friends, families, and whatever homes they had known. They were heading to an unknown future. The train cars were filled with the sounds of kids crying, although many were too scared or angry to cry, and just endured the journey.

Many of the Children's Aid Society orphans said they felt like cattle at each train stop. They were usually lined up on a courthouse lawn or on an auditorium stage to be examined by prospective parents who looked at their teeth and felt their limbs to make sure they were strong enough to work.

The movement lasted a total of 75 years, with the last train rolling to a stop in 1929. Trains ceased with the beginnings of the Great Depression. By this time, it is said some 250,000 children were "placed out." This period of mass relocation of children in the United States is widely recognized as the beginning of documented foster care in America. Many received good homes. Those who didn't fare so well at least had not been left on the street to die of hunger, or disease, or to become a crime statistic.

Numbers of children and poor families placed out from 1854 until 1910 by the Children's Aid Society (Taken from 1910 Annual Report of the C.A.S.)

From 1854 until 1910, the New York Children's Aid Society had taken 106,245 children and poor families scattered among the states listed. The "Free Home Placing Out" continued for 19 more years, ending in the early 1930's. During these last years many thousands more were sent out. This chart does not reflect children placed by:

* New York Founding Hospital
* New England Home For Little Wanderers
* New York Juvenile Asylum
* Chicago Home Society
* Minnesota Home Society
* Salvation Army

and many other placing agencies. The total may be as high as 200,000 placed, giving us an estimated number of 2,000,000 descendants of Orphan Train Riders living today.

Alabama	39	Idaho	52	Massachusetts	375	New Mexico	1	South Dakota	43

Alabama	39
Arkansas	136
California	168
Canada	566
Colorado	1,563
Connecticut	1,588
Delaware	833
Dist. Of Columbia	172
Florida	400
Georgia	317
Idaho	52
Illinois	9,172
Indian Territory	59
Indiana	3,955
Iowa	6,675
Kansas	4,150
Kentucky	212
Louisiana	79
Maine	43
Maryland	563
Massachusetts	375
Michigan	5,326
Minnesota	3,258
Mississippi	240
Missouri	6,088
Montana	83
Nebraska	3,442
Nevada	59
New Jersey	4,977
New York	33,053
New Mexico	1
New Hampshire	136
North Carolina	144
North Dakota	975
Ohio	7,272
Oklahoma	95
Oregon	90
Pennsylvania	2,679
Rhode Island	340
South Carolina	191
South Dakota	43
Tennessee	233
Texas	1,327
Utah	31
Vermont	262
Virginia	1,634
Washington	231
West Virginia	149
Wisconsin	2,750
Wyoming	19

vii

CHAPTER 1

Fred – Deceased Orphan Train rider from Clarks, Nebraska; brother of Howard.

Howard – Deceased rider from Stromsburg, Nebraska; brother of Fred.

Personal Interview with Fred:

Fred does not remember anything about his life until he stepped off the train in Nebraska at age six and was taken into a family to be their new son. "Mother Nature has a way of blanking out the bad things of your childhood," Fred always joked.

Fred is one of more than a quarter million children who were shipped from the East coast to be "adopted" by farm families in the Midwest. He was six years old when he boarded the train with his then three-year-old brother Howard.

Fred was never officially adopted by his Nebraska parents in Clarks, Nebraska, but he was always treated as their son, and even received an inheritance. He chose to take their last name and never had trouble using it until he was in the military overseas and needed a birth certificate to get home. It was only then that his Nebraska father went to the courthouse to legally change Freddie's last name.

Unfortunately, the love Fred received was not indicative of many Orphan Train riders' experiences. The orphans ranged in age from babies to 18 years old. Many were picked for their ability to work on a farm and were treated more like the animals than children. Some were forced to sleep in the barn and beaten if their work was unsatisfactory. Fred said he had talked to some orphans who had run away from their new homes and set out on their own at the tender age of 12 or 13.

Although representatives from the Children's Aid Society took care of the children and found them homes, and periodically checked on them, the system was not foolproof. Fred said some families would not let the children talk to the representatives, and other families threatened children if they did not promise to report that everything was okay.

The Orphan Trains ran from 1854-1929 and distributed orphaned and neglected children all over the rural areas of the country. Fred said some of the children were taken off the streets. Some were true orphans, and others were taken from homes where they were being abused or neglected. "I was taken from my parents for scandalous neglect," Fred said.

Many brothers and sisters were separated and never saw each other again. One child might have been "picked" by a family in one state only to have a sibling find another family in another state. One woman, Fred said, recently found her twin brother she had not seen in 60 years. Fortunately, for Fred, his brother lived with a family just 20 miles away. "We visited and got to play together just like you do with your cousins," Fred said, explaining he saw his brother several times a year.

When asked if he ever wanted to meet his real parents, who lived in New York, Fred said, "No!" He said that he did meet his father once. When asked if he forgave his biological parents, he said, "I never held anything against them."

Fred became a very close friend to this Author. He carried this verse in his billfold, as I do now:

"This is the road to tomorrow
And this is a place called today.
It's a wonderful place to visit,
But no one may ever stay."
– Author Unknown

Personal Interview with Howard's Daughter Renee:

Howard was only three years old when he was taken from his parents in Upstate New York in May 1925. He was so young that he did not remember much about his trip aboard the Orphan Train with his brother Fred. He was in three orphanages and four foster homes in six months' time. His fourth foster home in Stromsburg, Nebraska, became his permanent home. His foster father Roy, mother Martha, and sister Imogene were good to him.

He remembered only bits and pieces of the experience, but especially remembered a gift he received. It was a little red ball that had the alphabet all the way around!

As an adult, he served our country in WWII. He met his wife, Gladys, while he was a cab driver in New York.

Howard had given little thought to the Orphan Trains until invited to attend an Orphan Train Annual Celebration. The celebration renewed his interest, and he realized he should not let this very important part of history be swept under the rug. He traveled across the state of Nebraska dozens of times telling his story at schools, churches, and nursing homes.

By chance Howard won a computer in a grocery store drawing. When they called to tell him to pick up the computer, he thought they had the wrong number. He thought it was a computer repair shop and he told them he didn't own a computer! They said, "Well, you do now." Howard felt it so important to keep the Orphan Train history alive that he learned the computer and spent many hours working on it.

When his health began to fail, he sought out the Internet to continue spreading the word. He designed two Web pages on the subject, complete with music and photos, information on the Orphan Trains and celebrations, and links to other sites. He received an award for his marvelous websites from the State of Nebraska. Howard was also presented the Charles Loring Brace Award by the Orphan Train Heritage Society of America, Inc. Over a four-year time span he estimated that he had received 5,000 – 10,000 e-mails on the subject!

The computer is how the Author found out about Orphan Trains initially. Howard's website and a few telephone calls were how this entire project began! I surfed the Internet and stumbled upon his website, which then led me, step by step, on my 3,000-mile trek to each rider and descendant interviewed. Many people visit his two websites. The family quit keeping track of hits on the websites in 2001 when the two combined totaled a whopping 52,000 hits!

Fred and Howard have both passed away. As Fred would say, "This was a wonderful place to visit, but no one may ever stay." Both were such instrumental leaders in keeping the Orphan Train history alive with their school presentation boards and stories. As an author and professional speaker, I feel privileged to walk in their paths to carry on this legacy.

Howard, age 3

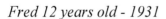

Fred 12 years old - 1931

Howard with his foster sister Imogene.

Martha, Howard, and Roy before Howard went into the service.

Fred just before going overseas - 1942

Howard in Hawaii - 1939

Howard with his foster family. (Left to Right) Roy, Imogene, Howard and Martha.

Howard and his milk truck!

Daughter-in-law Barbara with Fred by one of his program boards at annual Nebraska Orphan Train Celebration in Pawnee City, Nebraska.

Howard and wife Gladys with great-grandchildren Hallie, Brian, and Tanner.

7

Fred telling his Orphan Train Story at Springdale, Arkansas.

Fred ready for the Clarks, Nebraska, parade.

Fred and Lois (Chapter 10) at the Annual Nebraska Orphan Train Celebration in Broken Bow, Nebraska. This was the last photo of Fred. He passed away on May 9, 2005.

May 2000 - Howard telling his story at the Annual Nebraska Orphan Train Celebration in Aurora, Nebraska.

8

Howard, age 3; and Fred, age 6. Just off the Orphan Train in Osceola, Nebraska.

Howard and Fred – 75 years later in Osceola, Nebraska.

Fred and Howard's natural mother's grave in New York.

CHAPTER 2

Ralph – Deceased rider from Decatur, Nebraska.

Personal Interview with Ralph's Wife Mary:

Ralph was born on November 13, 1916, to Ralph and Edith. He was "boarded" by his mom in the home of a Mrs. Bland in New York City. His mom paid his board for a year and a half. Then she disappeared.

The age and birthplace of Ralph's parents were unknown, according to the Children's Aid Society, as was his dad's occupation.

When his mom stopped paying rent, efforts were made unsuccessfully to locate her. Relatives were contacted, but no clues as to her whereabouts were found, and on May 19, 1920, he was committed to the New York Nursery and Child's Hospital by the New York City Department of Welfare.

Ralph had no visitors while he was in the nursery so on September 13, 1922, he was referred to the Children's Aid Society. He was described as a "nice little fellow with freckles and brown hair." He was fine physically and mentally.

The Children's Aid Society received Ralph on October 2, 1922, and after three weeks at the Brace Farm School in Valhalla, New York, he went West via Orphan Train with their workers, Miss Bogardus and Miss Reynolds.

He was placed with a family at Tekamah, Nebraska, but, unfortunately, came down with the chicken pox, so was taken back to Tekamah, and left at a saloon to wait for Miss Bogardus and Miss Reynolds, who had gone on to Iowa and would be returning by train. Meanwhile Edith, a kindhearted resident at Tekamah, noticed the child in the unwholesome environment. She felt the saloon was no place for a child, and convinced her husband Charles they must take him home and away from such an atmosphere! Happily, Charles and Edith, who managed the Poor Farm in Tekamah, Nebraska, were approved as foster parents by the Agents. (Surprisingly, his stepmother held the same name as his natural mother.) They loved him from the start, and he was very happy with them. He had a dog, a bicycle, and a pony. He did well in school and was a great comfort to his foster parents, who had his last name changed legally to theirs, although they chose not to adopt him.

Despite Charles and Edith's encouragement to continue his schooling, Ralph quit school in 1932 when he was 16. He married Gwendolyn in 1934. Ralph and Gwendolyn had six children. They were divorced. In 1960 Ralph married Mary. Ralph and Mary celebrated 42 years of marriage. Ralph had three stepchildren. Ralph had many grandchildren, great-grandchildren, and great-great-grandchildren. Ralph passed away in May 2002.

Ralph - 1929

Ralph and wife Mary - 1996

CHAPTER 3

Lela – Rider from Columbus, Nebraska; sister of Melba and Aletha.

Melba – Deceased rider from Lincoln, Nebraska; sister of Lela and Aletha.

Aletha – Rider from Arizona; sister of Lela and Melba.

Personal Interview with Lela:

Lela of Columbus, Nebraska, has a story that differs from all the rest. While the majority of the children sent West on the Orphan Train were treated well, a few, including Lela, were taken by couples who wanted nothing more than a hired girl or slave.

Lela was just 2 ½ years old in 1917 when her parents put her in the Children's Aid Society. Her sister Melba was 1 ½. She was also put in the same orphanage. Her youngest sister, Aletha, was only 10 months old. She was put in the New York Foundling Hospital.

Unfortunately, Lela and Melba were not allowed to stay together as sisters. Lela's train ride West found her in a series of foster homes in Missouri and, finally, Nebraska. Moving from foster home to foster home she learned many lessons in life. She had been a city kid, and rural America was so new to her! Simple rural Missouri summer day activities such as playing in the mud under a huge windmill, squeezing mud up between her toes, then washing her feet off in a nice warm tub of clean water which the sun had warmed are memories fondly recalled by Lela. While living in the country, she experienced her first shopping trip to town. They went to stores; they bought dresses, shoes, and something very special, a Raggedy Ann doll. She just couldn't comprehend anyone buying her such nice, new things.

She never knew why she had to leave Missouri, but again she found herself on the Orphan Train, this time headed for Lincoln, Nebraska. December 5, 1920, was the day Lela arrived in Lincoln, which was to become her home for the next 83 years of her life. There she was placed with a woman who turned out to be abusive and controlling. "She told me I was a nobody," Lela said. "I was scared stiff of the woman; I was afraid all of the time! I'll always remember that day when, in her rage, she picked up my beloved Raggedy Ann doll and hurled it into the fire, and made me watch it burn. I was heartbroken!"

On December 5, 1933, she was married to her first love, John. He allowed her to escape the anxiety and fright that gripped her even on her wedding day. She recalls the day with a mixture of anguish and joy. "It was my wedding day, and my mother made me dust. When I missed a spot, she slapped me again and again!" Lela winced as she spoke.

After the birth of her son, she became more interested in her own heritage. Seeking to learn more of her background for herself and her son, Lela wrote to the Children's Aid Society. She found out that her parents had been alcoholics and were poor. When the children were brought to the orphanage, they were malnourished and scantily clothed. Lela has come a long, hard way, but she cherishes what she has learned from all of the trials and tribulations she went through.

Lela met her real father, brother, and four sisters in 1938. "I do not hold any grudges against my real parents," she said.

She has learned to give love and understanding. She has pity for poor, neglected children. She's a firm believer that one can overcome a negative situation with determination. She has chosen not be like her foster mother; she has chosen to be kind and loving. She has lots of love to give. She has chosen not to be mean! Life is a choice! If you learn from experience, like Lela, you'll follow the saying she keeps on the tip of her tongue, "Do unto others as you would have others do unto you!"

As an Author, I was fortunate to gain a very close friendship with Lela this past summer. For my *Plains Bound* professional speaking engagements and book signings, she helped my family develop a beautiful, handmade tablecloth that features many of the Orphan Train riders interviewed along my 3,000-mile journey. Lela and I attended the 2005 Orphan Train National Celebration in Concordia, Kansas, where she was one of the five riders in attendance to share her story. She loves to crochet and embroider. She makes her own unique greeting cards. She donates many of her wonderful handmade crafts to the annual Orphan Train Auction for the sake of keeping this important history alive.

Her husband John passed away in 1970 with cancer. He was in the hospital for four months. Lela sat beside his bed day and night. She took the vow "Until death do us part" and kept it.

Seven years later, Lela met a wonderful man named Paul. They were married on Mother's Day, May 8, 1977. On March 3, 1996, her second husband, Paul, passed away, also with cancer.

After 83 years of living in Lincoln, on February 1, 2002, she moved to Columbus, Nebraska, to be with her son and daughter-in-law. Lela spends her winters with a niece in Arizona where it's warmer. Besides crafts, she truly enjoys and has a love for nature, flowers, trees, and people. Lela has three grandchildren and eleven great-grandchildren.

Melba has passed away. Aletha resides in a nursing home in Arizona.

Lela's natural family in New York. (Left to Right – Back Row) Pernal, Pearl, Arnold; (Seated) Aletha, Joseph; (Left to Right – Front Row) Melba, Lela, Thelma.

Close-up of the wonderful handmade quilt made by 91-year old Lela.

Lela and daughter-in-law Elda display the magnificent Orphan Train quilt and pillow that Lela made and donated to the Annual National Orphan Train Auction at the Celebration in Concordia, Kansas.

Lela telling her Orphan Train story at the Annual National Orphan Train Celebration in Concordia, Kansas.

Lela diligently working on the Orphan Train tablecloth she helped the Author complete.

Lela and Charlotte developed a close friendship while working on the Orphan Train tablecloth that Charlotte uses in her speaking engagements and book signings.

CHAPTER 4

Mary "Red" — Deceased rider from Stuart, Nebraska.

Personal Interview with Mary's Niece Kathleen;
Mary's life story in her own words:

On December 12, 1912, I arrived at Stuart, Nebraska, along with five other children. These children were also left at Stuart. I was just 3 ½ at that time and was adopted by Herman and Sophia, whose family already included 11 living children. Three more had died in infancy.

As I grew older, I felt they truly wanted me. They were wonderful parents, and the seven brothers and four sisters were great. I was "little sis" to all of them. I learned my mother placed me in the New York Foundling Hospital when I was only two weeks old. She gave her name as Katie, but no reason for placing me in the home was ever given to me. My father may have been a man named James. Nothing at all is known of him.

Many orphans have tried to trace their roots, but I never really cared to know my ancestry when I was young. I was one of the very lucky ones. I didn't know why my parents were interested in adopting when they already had a large family. I think perhaps my parents were interested in having someone to care for them in old age. Mom told me she wanted a little girl with red hair, so they got me.

Even though there were so many in their family, and they were not wealthy people, they had the best thing in the world to give. That was LOVE. This Stuart family is my true family. They took me in when no one else wanted me. They fed, clothed, educated, and cared for me when I was sick.

After both of my parents died, I went to live on the farm with my sister Katie and her husband Frank. Over the years I worked in many homes taking care of new mothers and their babies. I also took care of older children, cooked meals, and performed other duties. On October 26, 1938, I married my husband Ed. After 9 ½ years, he was killed in an explosion in a home.

It had been a lifelong dream of mine to become a nurse, so I went to school and became a Licensed Practical Nurse. I worked in a home for the elderly in Illinois for 20 or more years. When I retired, I came home to Stuart to live with Kathleen, the wife of my nephew Francis.

Mary passed away January of 1992.

Mary fulfilled her dream of becoming a Licensed Practical Nurse!

Mary was a First Communion flower girl in 1915.

This was the maroon bonnet and light pink coat that Mary "Red" wore on the Orphan Train.

CHAPTER 5

James – Rider from Decatur, Nebraska; brother of Harry and Mary Ellen.

Harry – Deceased rider from Kearney, Nebraska; brother of James and Mary Ellen.

Mary Ellen – Deceased rider from Hornell, New York; sister of James and Harry.

Personal Interview with James:

James is 87 years old. My interview with him was just as heartwarming as I expected. He resides in Decatur, Nebraska. When he was about age seven, he came from New York on the Orphan Train with his sister Mary Ellen and brother Harry and at least 5,000 others to Nebraska. The three were sent to different homes in Nebraska.

Their mom died when Harry was born. Their dad just couldn't take care of all three of them. James lived in various foster homes starting in Overton, Nebraska. The first family had a son of their own who was just a baby. James lived with them for about one year. Lexington, Nebraska, was his next foster home. At Lexington, he was proud to be the "oldest" child in the family. With this label came the responsibility of helping on the farm. They had a steam engine. James' job was to watch the water gauge. In his childhood years James recalls living in Overton, Lexington, Grand Island, Loup City, Tekamah and, finally, Decatur, Nebraska. He smiles when he recalls his favorite pony which he rode three miles to school. It was a racehorse named "Babe"! "In those days we didn't miss school for a snowflake. We rode to school on our horses in 20-below-zero weather," James recalls.

He also had a bike which had been purchased from Sears, Roebuck and Company for $29.95! James says he wore it out riding it on a 50-mile bike ride to Omaha on Saturdays.

James feels he had a good childhood. Foster parents Gene and Lena, of rural Tekamah, had no children of their own, yet took James and a retarded boy named Charles into their home. James quit school a month before graduation from high school to serve our country. He's a veteran of 4 years and 28 days. He served in WWII with the Army Combat Engineers in Europe.

After he came home from WWII, he worked for Texseed. He worked in various cities and towns. He farmed for many years. When he retired he was building mobile homes in Tekamah, Nebraska. James was married to his beloved wife Alice for 61 years. She passed away in November of 2003. He has two daughters, Mary and Linda; five grandchildren; and six great-grandchildren.

His brother Harry was adopted in Kearney, Nebraska. His sister Mary Ellen was moved from Nebraska and later adopted in Hornell, New York. They also felt they had good childhoods. All three kept in touch throughout the years. Both Harry and Mary Ellen have passed away.

James with his racehorse "Babe" in 1936.

*(Left to Right) Harry, Mary Ellen, and James –
1969*

*May 30, 2005 - James at Author's
interview.*

(Left to Right) Mary, James, Alice, Linda

CHAPTER 6

William J. and Hannah McCully – He
served as a Superintendent at the Eighteenth Street Lodging House and the brand new Seventh Avenue Lodging House in New York, and as an Agent for the Orphan Trains. She served as Matron at the Eighteenth Street Lodging House and the brand new Seventh Avenue Lodging House in New York. When he became an Agent, they moved to Broughton, Kansas. Descendants were interviewed at Clay Center, Kansas.

Personal Interview with McCully Descendants Leo and Irene:

William J. McCully was Comptroller for the City of New York. This was a secure and well-paying job. He was an elected official. He reported the city's finances to the Mayor, City Council, and the people of New York City. However, he could see a need to help the poor children on the streets, so he teamed up with Charles Loring Brace and the Children's Aid Society.

Three years after their marriage, W.J. and Hannah McCully became the Superintendent and Matron for the Children's Aid Society's Eighteenth Street Lodging House. In 1884, brand new quarters were constructed for the children at Seventh Avenue and 32nd Street into which the McCullys also moved.

In 1885, Mr. Lyman took over Mr. McCully's position. This allowed Mr. McCully to work in the Western Placing Agency so that they could rear their family in a rural setting. William John McCully loved children, and when he was freed up to help in the Western Placing Agency, this meant that he could now become an Agent on the Orphan Train and help many children find homes as they traveled West. Mr. McCully was an Agent from 1885 – 1893. During that time frame he placed 960 children from New York into new homes via the Orphan Train!

Arthur Norton was a child Mr. McCully could not find a home for, so his wife Hannah kindly took him in. Older children such as he were very hard to place. He loved to read. He worked for a variety of farmers while he lived with the McCullys. He lived under the McCully roof until he was middle aged, when he moved out on his own to Ottawa, Kansas. The McCullys also had five children of their own.

William and Hannah lived in Broughton, Kansas, which no longer exists. It was a small town just southeast of Clay Center, Kansas. It was located in the Milford Dam project.

The McCully family remained close to the Brace family, with several generations of children named after Charles Loring Brace, the founder of the Children's Aid Society. William and Hannah have both passed away. They leave behind many descendants who also embrace keeping the Orphan Train history alive.

William John McCully

Hannah Johnston McCully

Wedding picture of William John McCully, age 31; and Hannah Johnston McCully, age 22.

Arthur Norton

July 25, 1913 - William and Hannah on a trip to San Francisco, California, after they retired.

(On this and the following three pages you'll see a replica of the report submitted by Mr. McCully of the very important work they were doing for 150 children at that time.)

THIRTY-SECOND

ANNUAL REPORT

OF THE

CHILDREN'S AID SOCIETY

1884

LODGING HOUSE OF THE CHILDREN'S AID SOCIETY
No. 400 SEVENTH AVENUE, CORNER 32d STREET.

NEW YORK:

ITALIAN SCHOOL PRINTING DEPARTMENT,
156-160 LEONARD STREET

1884

Author's Note: Please pay close attention to the very special people who maintained an active interest in the work of the Lodging House, furnishing bountiful dinners at the holidays, shirts and shoes at Christmas, and prizes for attendance and progress at night school. These gentlemen conducted the Sunday evening meetings for many years!

THIRTY-SECOND ANNUAL REPORT   1884

THE WEST SIDE LODGING HOUSE
No. 400 SEVENTH AVENUE, CORNER OF 32d STREET.

This Lodging House, one of the most commodious and picturesque buildings which the Society has thus far possessed, was the noble gift of Mr. J. J. ASTOR, erected this year. Its design, by Mr. C. VAUX, the architect, has been greatly admired for its practical and picturesque character. The building has proved very popular with the little rovers of the street, and every bed has been filled. A new Industrial School has been opened in it for the children from the tenement houses on the West side, under our devoted teachers, Miss HAIGHT and Mrs. BRYANT. This has begun with the usual difficulties from the wild habits and poverty of the children, but is sure to be a success.

(Extracts from the Annual Report of the Superintendent.)
With a feeling of pleasure and gratification we present our annual report, which shows the work of eight months in our old quarters and over three months in our new Home, corner of Seventh avenue and 32^d street.

The great need for such a building on the West side even our short experience here has fully shown. On June 26th we opened with **56** boys taken from 18th street, which number has steadily increased until at the present time there are **140** in the house, every bed being filled. The boys fully appreciate the beauties and comforts of their new Home.

The location is one of the best that could have been selected, being right on the ground where the Society's labors are perhaps as much needed as anywhere else in the city; gangs of rough fellows infest the neighborhood, and drunkenness and rioting prevail at all hours of the night. Whilst we cannot hope to benefit much those who have already grown beyond our reach, still we do hope to be able to exert some controlling influence over the younger boys.

A brief description of the house may be of some interest:

The building is of brick with sandstone trimmings 44 by 86 feet, five stories high, and is very beautiful in exterior. The entrances are in 32^d street. The first floor or basement contains boys' reception-room, play-room, water-closets, lavatory and bath-room, and a steam closet for dry-ing boys' clothing when they come in wet; in a separate division on the same floor are boiler-room, store-room, and laundry.

On the second floor are the boys' dining-room, kitchen, Superinten-dent's office, dining-room, kindergarten, and nursery.

On the third floor is the audience-room – a beautiful hall capable of seat-ing 400 persons – a teacher's room, and the living rooms of the Superin-tendent. The audience-room is used by the boys as a sitting-room, reading-room, and school-room, and here they have their private lockers, where their clothes, etc., are kept. It is also formed into two divisions by folding doors, and used as class-rooms during the day.

The fourth and fifth floors are used as dormitories, there being on each floor, and adjoining the main dormitory, a compartment for a few single beds, for which a little extra charge is made. The beds are all first-class, with iron frames and woven wire mattresses, and there is ample accom-modation for **150** boys.

The house is perfect in every respect, and admirably adapted to the work for which it is intended. It is at once a credit to the architect, and a monument to the philanthropy of its founder.

We have much to be thankful for in the possession of our beautiful new Home, yet with it come many additional responsibilities – a largely in-creased number of friendless and destitute boys are to be aided and pro-vided for, shoes and clothing will be needed in large quantities, and homes and work are to be found for many more, and we would earnestly call upon the friends of the poor boys to come to our assistance in the work. It is true that some may look repulsive, and not all seem grateful

for benefits bestowed, yet, as a rule, kind words and deeds are appreciated, and many a poor outcast has been reclaimed by kind and judicious
treatment. In this connection we would respectfully call to the attention
of those interested, the great good that could be accomplished through a
fund for starting boys in business. By this means boys could partly as-
sist in supporting themselves until a permanent home could be found,
and it would in a great measure prevent the boys from becoming thieves
or idle loungers. As our numbers are largely drawn from those tempo-
rarily out of employment, the importance of the "business fund" cannot
be over-estimated.

Mr. JAMES K. GRACIE, Messrs. ROOSEVELT, the sons of the late
THEODORE ROOSEVELT, and Mr. HILBORNE L. ROOSEVELT,
still maintain an active interest in the work of the lodging house, furnishing bountiful dinners at the holidays, shirts and shoes at Christmas, and
prizes for attendance and progress at night school. These gentlemen
have conducted our Sunday evening meetings for many years, and to
their earnest and faithful efforts much of the success attending the work
must be ascribed. Many reports have been received from former inmates
who are successfully fighting the battle of life.

If our work in the past has been in any measure satisfactory and encouraging, considering the many disadvantages under which we labored,
may we not confidently predict a grand and useful future for the new
lodging house?

THIRTY-SECOND ANNUAL REPORT   1884

EXPENSES AND RECEIPTS

Total expenses...$11,533.14
Deduct construction and outfit................................. 5,675.86

Net expenses...$ 5,857.28
Deduct receipts...$ 3,750.62

Net Cost..$ 2,106.66

Respectfully submitted,

W. J. McCully,

Superintendent.

CHAPTER 7

Lester – Rider from Humboldt, Nebraska; brother of Lawrence, Marie, and Elsie; friend of Catherine (Lila).

Lawrence – Deceased rider from Osceola, Nebraska; brother of Lester, Marie, and Elsie.

Marie – Deceased rider from Gresham, Nebraska; sister of Lester, Lawrence, and Elsie.

Elsie – Deceased sister who remained in New York; sibling of Lester, Lawrence, and Marie.

Catherine (Lila) – Deceased fellow Orphan Train rider and former neighbor of Lester at Osceola, Nebraska.

Personal Interview with Lester:

Lester's interview, especially, intrigued me because although he's never officially published his works, he's a Nebraska author, too. Lester writes wonderful poetry. On our very first visit he so kindly shared with me an unpublished book of poems he had written from the heart entitled *Thoughts from the Pen of the Country Poet*. In this next poem, you'll see how he vividly explains his own experience as an orphan at the tender age of five:

ORPHAN TRAIN

You've heard about the children
Coming West upon the rail,
But when you know their story
Your troubles seem to pale.

Their eyes were filled with bitter tears.
Their hearts were filled with pain,
But they were the lucky ones;
They rode the Orphan Train.

They came from doors and benches
Of the streets on which they roam
Abandoned by their family
No place to call their home.

Then by fate, or maybe luck
Some one came and eased their pain.
The chosen ones headed West
Aboard the Orphan Train.

Not knowing where or even when
They would finally find a place
To settle down and call it home
The beginning of life's race.

Family ties were broken now;
They went where they were sent.
The lucky ones knew the place
Where they said they went.
The rest of us just stood the strain
Of months aboard that Orphan Train.

Bad blood was the usual statement
The adults all seemed to say.
The children seemed to like us,
We'd run and laugh and play.

Most of them survived the test;

They proved the people wrong
Before the light of life had faded
And they wrote their final song.

So now you know the story
Of kids on a trip of pain.
Doctors, lawyers, and many such
All rode that Orphan Train.

His mom Bessie and dad John had separated in Allegany County, New York. On April 5, 1925, all four children were given to the orphanage. Lawrence was ten, Elsie was seven, Lester was five, and Marie was two. Lester's family was broken up immediately.

All but Elsie were put on the Orphan Train. She was hearing impaired and remained in New York. Eight children were on the car. Lester refuses to call them trains. Some of the cars were cattle cars lined with cardboard. Alice A. Bogardus from Lincoln, Nebraska, was the Agent with the children on the trip. People interested in the children were waiting at the Courthouse in Osceola, Nebraska. Lester can remember only the courthouse lawn where they were taken. The children on the train were not tagged, since they were with the Children's Aid Society, not the Sisters of Charity.

Six of the eight children were placed. **Harold**, age four, went to Osceola, Nebraska; **Fred**, age six (from Chapter 1), went to Clarks, Nebraska; **Howard**, age three (from Chapter 1), went to Stromsburg, Nebraska; **Catherine** (name later changed to Lila), age nine, went to Osceola, Nebraska, and was taken to a family that lived about a half mile from Lester. Lester's sister **Marie** was placed in Gresham, Nebraska. Lester's brother **Lawrence** was placed with a family in Osceola, Nebraska. **Lester** and **Isabelle** were not immediately chosen.

Although Lester wasn't initially chosen on the Courthouse lawn, Miss Bogardus knocked on doors until she came to Floyd and Mary, who took him in. Isabelle, age four, was not placed and her whereabouts are unknown to the Author. Lawrence's placement with his new family didn't work out. Coincidentally, on February 1, 1929, the new agent, Mrs. Swan, of Lincoln, Nebraska, brought him to the home where Lester lived. Floyd and Mary agreed to take him and welcomed him into the family. Thus, the brothers were allowed to grow up together after all!

Lester and Lawrence were not "adopted" but just "raised" until they were through school and on their own. Because they were foster children, the Children's Aid Society kept check on them. Lester remembers that Mrs. J. W. Swan replaced Mary and Alice A. Bogardus. She was replaced by R. L. Weatherly who, in turn, was replaced by Lora Lasch.

In 1937, after graduation from high school, Lester went to Lincoln, Nebraska, under the supervision of Mrs. Swan. After a few months he went to Omaha, Nebraska, under the supervision of Lora Lasch. He did a variety of jobs to make money. He worked as a chauffeur and a deliveryman. He worked on a dairy farm and at a dry cleaning establishment.

When Lester was 19, he joined the Civilian Conservation Corps (CCC). President Roosevelt came up with the idea to have the Civilian Conservation Corps or CCC for unemployed young men. Men who worked in these Corps were paid from $30 - $45 per month for their services, with 75% of their wages sent home to their parents. There were five camps in Nebraska. Lester worked in one of them.

Nebraska was part of an area termed the Seventh Corps Area made up of Arkansas, Iowa, Kansas, Minnesota, Missouri, North and South Dakota. This area consisted of about 30,000 men! Work entailed constructing telephone lines, truck trails, footpaths, buildings, dams, and fences for farmers. Lester recalls most of his time in the CCC was spent building fences, and clearing and planting trees. He eventually worked his way up to being a night watchman for the camp. He would watch over the camp at night while the other men slept. He would then sleep during the day while they worked!

After fulfilling his duties with the CCC, he went to work with the O. A. Cooper Company at Humboldt, Nebraska. He took two years off to join the Navy and be a radar man. He then returned to Humboldt, Nebraska, and returned to his job at the Cooper Company.

The Cooper Company specialized in all-purpose flour, pancake and waffle mix, biscuit mix, and flour for fish batter. They had three feed mills and a flour mill; therefore, Lester learned to do many things. He eventually became head miller. (A miller is a person who grinds grain into flour.) When Lester was age 62, the Cooper Company was sold. Lester's position was restructured so he became self-employed. He started his own repair shop. He began making many different yard ornaments. He still works in the shop at times and takes orders for items on demand. A person once asked Lester if he could do anything. He replied, "I don't know; I haven't tried it yet!"

Lester was married on May 13, 1939. He and his wife Margaret have lived in the Humboldt area for 66 years. They have four sons, seven grandchildren, and five great-grandchildren. Lester loves working with kids. Lester was a Scoutmaster for approximately 10 years in the Humboldt, Nebraska, area. This area has produced many Eagle Scouts. He was also an enthusiastic sponsor for the Methodist Youth Fellowship.

Lester was very close to his foster parents. His father passed away at age 96 and his mother, at age 90. During their last years, Lester served as their conservator (person responsible for their care) until they passed away.

We all like to hear stories of "How far did you go to school?" Lester went to country school. He walked 1/4 mile from his home in Osceola, Nebraska. High School was a little farther. He got there by horse and buggy or walked the 4 1/2 miles.

His foster mother Mary kept a wonderful diary and photo album for Lester that he shared with me. Here are a few of her interesting entries:

"December 25: I told him that someone had no children. He replied, 'Lonesome like you until you got me.'

"September 6: Lester's 7th birthday. Second term of school. Mrs. Fentress, teacher.

"September 30, Friday: Lester said, 'Hello, Sweetie,' to me as he came in the door.

"October 19, Tuesday, 1926: Family discussed stealing at the table. Lester said, 'They get theifer and theifer.'

"October 20, Wednesday: James hit Lester on the head with a clod. Christie brought him home, face covered with blood."

Mary discovered history repeated itself in her family. Perhaps the reason Mary kept such a remarkable record of the boys' lives was that she discovered her father had also come to the West on the Orphan Train and, sadly, he had few mementos of his past. During her research, she received a letter from the Children's Aid Society dated September 11,

1926. In it she was informed her father and his two brothers were sent West by the same Society on January 14, 1868! They came to the Society from an institution on Randall's Island, New York City, where they had been admitted on April 8, 1867, when her father was six years old. His brother Charles was ten and Thomas was eight. The grandfather's name was also Thomas. He was born in New York. The grandmother's name was Ellen. She was born in Scotland. The grandfather was a blacksmith and the grandmother was a milliner (a maker of women's hats). Their address was 243 Monroe Street in New York City. Her taking in two orphans completed a cycle of love and kindness.

Lester feels the Orphan Train was as good as the current adoption system. If Mary and Floyd would have been forced to pay today's adoption costs, Lester and Lawrence would probably not have had a home. They always had food to eat and were well cared for. "What else can you ask for?" Lester exclaims! "Money does not make a home or love."

I'll always recall Lester as the "Country Poet." I've read and enjoyed his many wonderful poems. He granted permission for me to share a few of them with you. I'm sure you'll enjoy them as much as I have. It's amazing how he can take a very simple subject and create such vivid images with words!

THE FIRST ROBIN

Oh poor little Robin
Shivering with cold,
I can't help but wonder
How you'd be so bold,
To make your way North
Thru the winds icy blast,
Except just to tell us
That winter won't last.

Cheer up little Robin
Your time will soon come,
To bask in the rays
Of the warm summer sun.
You'll soon find a mate
And build you a home,

For the balance of summer
No more to roam.

Just think, Little Robin
The time is now nigh,
You'll sit in the garden
With sharp eager eye,
You'll be watching and waiting
Without any sound,
For any small sign
Of worms in the ground.

Good Luck, Little Robin
You tell from the signs,
No cold winter wind
Will whistle the pines.
We all wish to thank you
As you travel your ways,
To spread the glad tidings
Of Winter's last days.

FRESH OILED ROAD

How many have noticed
A fresh oiled street,
It makes a mess of your tires
And sticks to your feet.

You rant and rave
As you try to remove,
The black slimy stuff
From every small groove.

But you never noticed
There is another side too,
Just listen a while
I'll tell it to you.
Walk down that street
While it is all wet,
And you'll be surprised
At the pleasure you'll get.

Keep your eyes on the ground
And to your surprise,
All the rainbows in heaven
Are in front of your eyes.

Green, blue, and purple
The colors unfold,
And crossing their border
Runs a river of gold.

It may be unusual
But it will lighten your load,
If you can find beauty
In a freshly oiled road.

MODERN GIRL

I know a nice young lady
And boy she's really sweet,
She's really something special
She's a girl you've got to meet.

When there is something that she wants
She usually gets her way,
You watch her and you'll never know
What she'll do from day to day.

When she starts the stove to cook
She needs a scene director,
If she doesn't then you know
She'll cook by smoke detector....

FORGOTTEN

They sit alone in silence
As the day drifts slowly by,
Here and there around the room
A tear will fill their eye.

Mothers, fathers and other ones
Have been left alone to stare,
At a place there on yonder wall
From their lonely wheel chair.

Let's not forget these lonely ones
As they pass their final days,

The old folks really need us
In so very many ways.

Try to make life a little better
With a card or just a word,
Not only will you feel better
I know your words are heard.

Here's a toast to all the old folks
May they enjoy their last days,
Whatever you can do for them
Comes back in many ways.

FIFTEEN BELOW

I rise in the morning
The clock says it's six,
I've sidewalks to scoop
And breakfast to fix.

As I peek out the window
I suddenly know,
It's a cool, cold morning
At fifteen below.
I put on my coat
And cursing my fate,
I shovel the sidewalk
Out to our front gate.

I get breakfast quickly
For to work I must go,
It's a very cold morning
At fifteen below.

I run to the car
The ending is blunt,
I step on the starter
All I get is a grunt.

I mustn't be late
And wouldn't you know,
The temperature's standing
At fifteen below.

As I get out to walk
My mind wanders back,
To when I was driving
Along this same track.

How well I remember
The summer's bright glow.
And the temperature wasn't

At fifteen below.

Cans, bottles and trash
They littered the gravel,
On the sides of the road
That I must now travel.

Then I'm roughly brought back
From the sun's summer glow,
My fingers are screaming
It's fifteen below.
I raise my eyes as the sun's early light
Turns the mantle draped trees into curtains of
White, as I look around me,
Why wouldn't you know, God created beauty
At fifteen below.

NUTS

I am looking for assistance
As I go up my way,
I would like to have someone explain
Why I dig from day to day.

The Season says that it's the time
To get the garden started,
But I'd just like to stop and say
It's time that we two parted.

You dig and hoe and plant the seeds
And wait for them to grow,
Then you have to pull the weeds,
To find just what you sowed.

Then at last the day arrives
And you can pick the crop,
The whole thing starts up again
Just when you think it stopped.

You hull and string
And heat and can,
And burn your little fingers
Upon that cooking pan.

Then you have the product
By then you're really proud,
You're sitting there all by yourself
On your little lacy cloud.

You go to the Super Market
And do you get a drag,
As you read the 29 cents
Written on the tag.

Lester wrote many poems for loved ones for special occasions. This is my favorite one; I'm certain you will enjoy it. This is the poem he wrote to his wife for their 50th wedding anniversary:

THE ROSE

While traveling along life's path,
And living day to day,
I came upon a tender bud
That made me want to stay.

As the months went slowly by
The bud began to grow,
And as the bloom begins to spread
It must be mine I know.

Now the months have turned to years
In full blossom is the Rose,
And as the sands of time run by
We'll reap just what it sows.

Now the Rose begins to fade
In other eyes but mine,
But I'll care for that tender bud
While I still have the time.

Life must be lived upon this earth
On this we'll all agree,
And we'll enjoy what we have left
My budding Rose and me.

Although Lester's mother was exceptionally disciplined in her writing and kept wonderful records of the brothers growing up, Lester credits his interest in writing to his foster father Floyd's influence.

His father liked to write poems for his own enjoyment. They never attracted much attention except for one poem that became quite popular. It was a great surprise when Lester revealed to me that the words to the popular holiday song "Jolly Old St. Nicholas" were written by none other than his foster father Floyd.

It appears that at one time the poem was submitted for consideration and possible publication but nothing ever happened as a result. No answer was received even though we know that at some point someone put the poem to music and the song appeared in songbooks with no credits given for either the words or the music. Thus Lester's father never received the recognition he deserved for this popular bit of verse. Floyd was so discouraged he never wrote another poem.

JOLLY OLD ST. NICHOLAS

Jolly old St. Nicholas, lend your ear this way
Don't you tell a single soul, what I'm going to say
Christmas Eve is coming soon
Now you dear old man,
Tell me what you bring to me
Whisper if you can.
When the clock is striking twelve
When I'm fast asleep,
Down the chimney, broad and black
With your pack you creep.
All the stockings you will find
Hanging in a row,
Mine will be the shortest one
So you'll be sure to know.
Johnny wants a pair of skates
Susie wants a dolly,
Nellie wants a story book
She thinks that dolls are folly,

As for me, my brain I fear
Isn't very bright,
Choose for me dear Santa Claus
What you think is right.

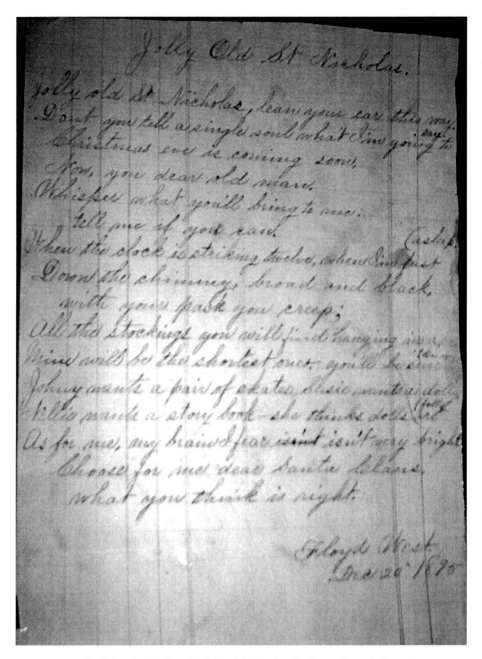

Original "Jolly Old St. Nicholas" signed and dated December 20, 1895, by Lester and Lawrence's foster father Floyd.

Lester and Lawrence's foster father, Floyd, author of "Jolly Old St. Nicholas" dated December 20, 1895.

Lester – 1928

Lester at work in the mill.

Lester married Margaret in Seneca, Kansas, on May 13, 1939.

Lester (on horse) and Lawrence (by plow).

Lawrence and Marie – 1938

*Lester out for a
Sunday visit to see
his brother Lawrence
when they still lived
in separate homes in
Nebraska. - 1927*

*Neighbor and fellow
Orphan Train rider,
Catherine (Lila).*

Lester, Lawrence, Marie, and Elsie's natural father, John, from New York – 1935.

Alice A. Bogardus of Lincoln, Nebraska. She passed away on December 7, 1925, at the age of 60.

Catherine (Lila) – April 1933

May 26, 2005 – Lester at Author's interview.

Lester and his foster mother Mary.

CHAPTER 8

Paul – Rider from Lindsay, Nebraska.

Personal Interview with Paul and His Nephew Fred:

Reverend Paul as a boy was one of some 250,000 youths who traveled to the Midwest from the New York City area on an Orphan Train. The Reverend, at about age three, was to ride on one of the last Orphan Trains in 1929, after which the practice was disbanded.

The Reverend refers to his childhood as a great one. He wanted to make his parents proud and so he became a priest. He explains he had a wonderful home with his mom Anna and dad Andrew in Raeville, Nebraska. He was their only child and admits he was probably "spoiled rotten." He walked across the field to school, and helped with the typical farm chores.

He attended Raeville Grade School and High School and graduated from St. John's Bercham in 1940. He attended St. Lawrence College, Mount Calvary, Wisconsin, for three years, taking his philosophy course at St. Louis Preparatory Seminary, St. Louis, Missouri. He especially enjoyed his time at the St. Louis Seminary. He completed his theological courses at Kenrick Seminary in St. Louis and was ordained on April 25, 1949.

Over the years he was assigned to many churches. He has served parishes at Randolph, Omaha, St. Anthony's, rural Platte Center, St. John's, Lindsay, Clarks, Primrose, and Butte, Nebraska.

In 1979, Reverend Paul officiated at the funeral of fellow Orphan Train rider, Catherine (in Chapter 11). Over the years, he was instrumental in hosting and organizing Orphan Train celebrations of persons like himself, commemorating the journeys made to new homes in Nebraska during the early 1900's. Friends from near and far attended these celebrations, which were started by former orphans from the old New York Foundling Hospital.

In 1987, he was instrumental in including the Children's Aid Society in the Nebraska Annual Celebrations. Reverend Paul added the Celebration of Mass to the festivities of the many celebrations he attended over the years. As part of the service on the first weekend in May 1988, an orphan from Everett, Washington, and his wife renewed their marriage vows. The couple was observing their 51st wedding anniversary.

Reverend Paul's health is failing to the point that he is no longer able to attend the annual celebrations that he was once so influential in organizing.

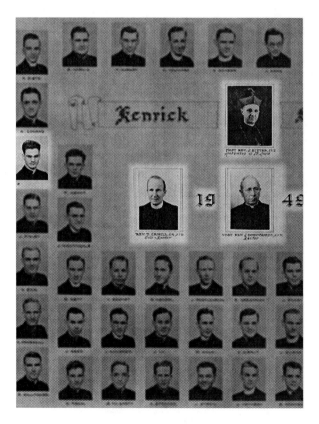

(First Column, Row 3) Paul graduated in 1949.

Father Paul's first Mass.

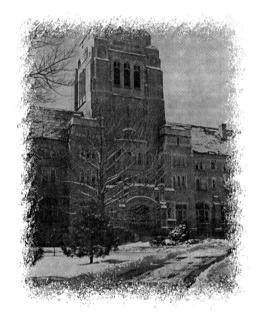

January 1944 - Kendrick Seminary in St. Louis, Missouri.

*June 16, 2005 –
Father Paul at
Author's interview.*

CHAPTER 9

Charles - Deceased rider from Atkinson, Nebraska.

Personal Interview with Charles' Sister Clara:

ORPHANS BROUGHT TO NEBRASKA FROM NEW YORK

Between 1854-1929 Orphan Train documentation is sketchy, but estimates say that roughly anywhere between 150,000 – 250,000 orphans left New York on trains.

The Bishop from Omaha in 1912 notified his parishes in Nebraska that the New York Foundling Hospital was overcrowded. They were looking for homes for some of these babies and children. Some of these children had been left orphans by the sinking of the Titanic, the loss of a father, or for various other reasons.

The people in the Stuart and Atkinson, Nebraska, area responded to the Bishop's call, and a few months later a train with three coaches, filled to capacity with these orphans, left New York. They were cared for on the journey by a priest and several nuns of the Sisters of Charity Order who operated the orphanage.

These homeless and neglected children were placed in homes throughout the Midwest. Many children found homes in Nebraska. Sixteen came to Holt County, Nebraska.

Each child wore a number pinned to him for identification, and when children were accepted by their new parents, papers corresponding to their numbers were given to the adopting parents.

Charles was adopted at age two by Karl and Theresa in 1912, after they had had several miscarriages. He was their oldest. After adopting him, they had eight more children of their own.

All he knew of his background from New York was that his dad had died and his mom was not in good health. He didn't know if he had brothers or sisters back in New York.

In 1962, the 50th Annual Orphan Train Celebration was held in Grand Island, Nebraska. Sixty-five former orphans attended; these were orphans that had been brought to Nebraska from the New York Foundling Hospital. Some of those attending came from as far away as Montana and Illinois. At this time it was learned that seven of the orphans had become nuns and two had entered the priesthood. Father Paul, a former Assistant Pastor at St. Joseph Church at Atkinson (Chapter 8), was in attendance at this celebration. He had come to Nebraska as one of these orphans.

Many of the sixteen who came to Holt County were successful throughout the years in tracing their ancestry and knew some of the circumstances surrounding their adoption. Most of the children grew to adulthood in the community into which they had been adopted and, for most, life was wonderful. Only one incident of tragedy has been attached to any one of this group—one woman was murdered in 1954. Charles has passed away. All of the original riders who remained in the Holt County area have also passed away.

Photo taken of Charles about the time he was adopted by Karl and Theresa – 1912.

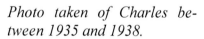

Photo taken of Charles between 1935 and 1938.

CHAPTER 10

Lois – Rider from Broken Bow, Nebraska; sister of Muriel (Merle) and Irene.

Muriel (Merle) – Rider from Fort Morgan, Colorado; Author met her at Concordia, Kansas; sister of Lois and Irene.

Irene – Deceased rider from Arkansas; sister of Lois and Merle.

Personal Interview with Sisters Lois and Merle:

The three sisters were born in Suffolk County, Long Island, New York. Due to an influenza epidemic, their mother Lorena was left widowed. She was burdened with four young daughters to raise. Destitute, in poor health, and recognizing that she could not care for her daughters, she surrendered three of her children. The girls, ranging in age from 15 months to nine years old, were subsequently turned over to the Children's Aid Society of New York City. They lived in the care of the Society for six weeks. On the morning of June 19, 1923, Lois, Muriel, and Irene boarded a Westbound Orphan Train along with 29 other children under the supervision of the Society's Miss Bogardus. Their final destination was an orphanage in Omaha, Nebraska.

The girls did not remain together. Irene was placed in a home without her sisters. Muriel and Lois were placed initially with a family in Washington County, Nebraska. Their adopted father was a prosperous miller. The family had a 19-year-old daughter. In December of 1923, the family decided they wanted a boy. They asked the Society to take back one of the sisters. Subsequently, Lois was placed with another family in Washington County, Nebraska.

Lois's life story in her own words:

My foster parents owned a general store in DeSoto, Nebraska. They sold it and moved to Blair, Nebraska, where they later adopted me. My adopted folks changed my last name. I was one of the lucky children! They adopted me in December of 1923 at Blair, Nebraska. Erna was my adopted mother's name. She was a piano teacher. My father was a rural mail carrier. His name was Clyde.

We lived in a big white house on Nebraska Street on the edge of town. The house was pretty large, and it was very nice. I remember having a big storm come through Blair, and the wind blew the chimney off the house! The storm scared me! I sat on my mother's lap the whole time it was storming. I also remember as a child receiving a doll and a doll buggy for Christmas. We always had a Christmas tree at Christmastime.

When I was a little girl, we had chickens, a couple of horses that my dad used to pull a buggy with, and we also had a mother pig with six little piglets. Sometimes I helped feed the chickens.

Dad sold the big house, and we moved to West Lincoln Street in Blair. The second house was smaller but nice.

I had one really good friend named Edith. She lived across the street from me. We played together all the time with our dollies. Her family was from Denmark. Edith and her family decided they didn't want to stay in America any longer, so they moved back to Denmark.

I went to school at North Ward Elementary in Blair. It was only a half block from my house, and I could walk to school every day.

My folks went on several trips. We went to the lakes in Iowa. They also took me to Minnesota and South Dakota.

I went to high school in Blair until my father had a massive heart attack. Then I quit school and helped him around the mail route, because his route was out in the country. The doctor told him he could continue his work if he had someone to accompany him. So I went with him every day!

We had some good times and some bad times, but we had a good home life.

I worked in Florence and Omaha, Nebraska, for a few years as a nanny. This is when I met my husband Robert from Wahoo, Nebraska. We dated for a while and decided to get married on March 22, 1941. We celebrated 64 years of wedded bliss this year.

My husband was in the dirt business; he drove heavy machinery. We have lived all over the country: Colorado, Georgia, New Mexico, Kansas, Nebraska, Louisiana, Oklahoma, and a few other states. We have 3 children, 5 grandchildren, 11 great-grandchildren, and 2 great-great-grandchildren. My family organized the 2005 Annual Nebraska Orphan Train Celebration in Broken Bow, Nebraska. At the time of publishing, I am the sole Orphan Train rider attending statewide events. This is the life story of one little orphan girl who was loved and cared for by parents who were wonderful.

Muriel's life story as told by her daughter Anita:

In March of 1924, a conflict emerged when Muriel's adopted mother indicated that she did not want Muriel to visit her sisters Lois and Irene. The Children's Aid Society disagreed and insisted that the girls continue to see each other. The family then sued the Society, and Miss Bogardus removed Muriel from the home and placed her with a new family.

The new couple was a childless couple in their fifties, and the Society felt they could provide a proper upbringing for young Muriel. They were very willing to let the sisters visit each other. They changed Muriel's name to Merle Elizabeth and lovingly welcomed her into their family. William Edgar (Ed) was a farmer and Fannie, a retired schoolteacher. Due to Fannie's continuing health problems, the family left Nebraska in 1926 and relocated to a farm in Colorado.

Fannie died in 1932, leaving Ed with an 11-year-old daughter to rear. Merle became responsible for doing household duties and helping her dad run the farm. Ed believed in the philosophy, "Hands to Work, Hearts to God." Ed and Merle were very active in their church and often sang duets during services.

In 1941, Merle married. Ed left the farm and moved in with the young couple when they settled in town. Merle and her husband were blessed with three children. Her husband died in 1953 leaving her widowed at age 32. To support her family, she took in ironing and did cleaning at a local rooming house to supplement her meager Social Security check. She tenderly cared for her father until his death in 1963. Her youngest son died in 1990.

Her birth mother, Lorena, began writing to Merle when she was 18. Although the two maintained occasional contact until Lorena's death in 1981, Merle learned nothing about her father or the circumstances surrounding her removal from her original home. It just wasn't talked about. Lorena had remarried and had given birth to two sons. The youngest son, Leslie, was a fireman. He was killed in an accident before Merle had an opportunity to meet him. The remaining son, LeRoy, lives in New York, and Merle and her family have visited him on a number of occasions. They maintain a close relationship.

In 1968, Merle began working in a friend's drapery shop. Ten years later, she bought the shop and continued to operate it until ill health forced her retirement at age 84.

In spite of many difficult times throughout her life, Merle considers herself blessed. Ed and Fannie loved her, treated her kindly, and she was able to maintain contact with her sisters through the years. Family has always been an integral part of her life.

Resumed Personal Interview with Sisters Lois and Merle:

Irene was never adopted. She lived in a foster home all her life until she was married. Her sisters lived in the same town while growing up, but never recall seeing Irene at all, even though they may have unknowingly bumped into her at times. Irene married and had one child. Irene died in Arkansas in 1997.

Their baby sister, Eunice, who was kept by Lorena at the time the other three were given to the Children's Aid Society, remained in New York. She passed away in November of 2005.

63

For an author, it was an incredible opportunity to chat with two sisters who rode the Orphan Train together. They have faced difficult times in their lives with grace, dignity, and a strong, abiding faith. They have provided a wonderful legacy for their families. I have grown to know them as women of integrity and courage whom I admire a great deal. Their shared enthusiasm and zest for life can be summed up in a quote by Merle, "Each day is a gift from God, full of surprise, and I don't intend to miss a single one!"

Lois – 11 months

Irene

Merle, age 3

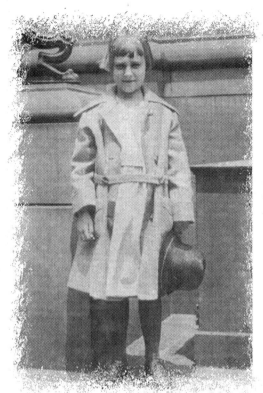

Irene, age 9

Lois in Blair, Nebraska, with her favorite doll buggy.

Lois, age 6

Irene and Lois

Lois in front of her house in Blair, Nebraska, wearing the red cape her mom bought for her.

Lois and her adopted mom, Erna.

Muriel (Merle)

Lois in New York.

Lois and Charlotte find the "perfect" china head dolls for when Charlotte portrays Lois in the Orphan Train talk.

June 11, 2005 - Merle and Lois at Author's interview.

Merle at 2005 National Orphan Train Celebration at Concordia, Kansas.

CHAPTER 11

Catherine – Deceased rider from Beemer, Nebraska. Author interviewed her daughter of Lincoln, Nebraska, and her son of Beemer, Nebraska.

While in high school, Catherine's grandson Mitch wrote a profile of his beloved grandmother who passed away when he was age ten. He has graciously shared his tribute with us to further clarify this era of American History:

"A Profile: My Grandmother"

"My grandmother was a great person. She was one of those people that you think of as a grandmother. She always wanted a hug and a kiss when you walked through the door. She was one of the best persons there ever was. This is her biography.

"Catherine was born on November 14, 1910. She was born in Brooklyn, New York. Her original parents baptized her on November 22, 1910. On December 15, 1910, she was taken to the New York Foundling Hospital where her mother left her in care of the nuns there because the family could not take care of her. Later it was found out that she had four brothers and sisters that were living. The evidence of her brothers and sisters was found on her birth certificate.

"Catherine lived in the Foundling Hospital until she was 1 ½ years old. She was then placed on the Orphan Train like many other orphans had been when they were children so they could find a better home in the West. Catherine went from New York City to West Point, Nebraska. In

West Point, Nebraska, Ferdinand and Mary Anna picked her up. They were looking for a child just like her. The rather odd thing about this was that they already had 17 children of their own, none of which were adopted.

"Catherine was not adopted at this time, she was indentured. Indentured means that she lived with the family almost as a foster child. Then at the age of 18 the family could adopt her. Anytime before that she could be returned for any reason.

"Ferdinand and Mary Anna were good parents. They treated Catherine better than just a regular child. Catherine lived with them and their children, which were still at home. Many of which had moved out. She grew up in West Point, Nebraska. All of the children took care of her and loved her like a natural born sister.

"Catherine never found anything out about her original family. Her daughter, Kathleen, looked into the matter and found her original parents names and background. Catherine's father's name was William. He was born in the United States and was an engineer. Her mother's name was also Catherine. She was born in Canada and was 44 when her daughter Catherine was born. When Catherine, the daughter, was 17 she tried looking into her background. She gave up searching for one reason – she thought she might make her new family think they were not good enough for her. This was quite the contrary, so she did not go any further. A second reason Catherine gave up the search was the lack of finding any additional information. Catherine was looking in Manhattan, New York City, when she was actually born in Brooklyn, New York City.

"Catherine's indentured father, was born in Germany on August 29, 1842. Her indentured mother, Mary Anna, was evidently born in the United States in 1859. Ferdinand came to the United States in 1868. Ferdinand died in 1926 when Catherine was only 16 years old. At this time, she could have been sent back to the Foundling Hospital but being the caring family they were, her sisters took care of her. At this time the priest of the Catholic Church sent her to Carroll, Iowa, to get a good High School education and it was there that she graduated.

"After she graduated she came back to West Point, Nebraska. Catherine then worked at the Hotel. She loved to dance and dancing is how she met Joe. She met Joe when she was 22 years old. Two years after dating him they were married. The wedding date was June 11, 1934. Their first child was born that following August. When asked why they waited so long to marry, Joe replied, 'Catherine wanted a June wedding.' In January 1936 their second child JoAnn was born. This was during an awful blizzard. The blizzard was said to be so bad that Joe and 20 other men walked from West Point to Oakland, Nebraska (a walk of about 20 miles) to break the crust of the snow in front of the road maintainer so that it could clear the road. That year, 1936, Joe and Catherine, moved to Houston, Texas. They moved to Houston in search of work. This is where a sister and a brother of Catherine's lived. They moved back to Nebraska after Catherine grew homesick. They then lived in Beemer, Nebraska. Joe now was working for the W.P.A. This was a great program set up for people who needed work. The program was made to put in power lines to get electricity into the rural areas. During this time, Clarence, their third child was born. They moved to North Platte, Nebraska for a short period of time.

"Joe and Catherine then moved back to Beemer where they lived from then on this time. Joe started working for a cattle feeder for whom he has been working forever since December 1942. Joe was supposed to go to war but a priest fought it because Catherine was pregnant with Kathleen, my mother. The priest won and Joe was able to stay home. After this time there were two more children born, LeRoy and Debra.

"Catherine then became very active in the community. Everyone knew her and she was well liked. In 1962 they had the first Orphan Train Celebration for the area. In 1978, when the celebration was held in Beemer, 49 orphans attended.

"On December 18, 1979, Catherine died from when she found out she had acute leukemia. She left her husband and many grandchildren behind. A fellow orphan spoke at the funeral, Reverend Paul of Primrose, Nebraska."

Mitch

Personal Interview with Catherine's Daughter Kathleen and Son Clarence:

Kathleen has a love for the Orphan Train history. Her mother passed away in 1979. Kathleen had to send copies of her own birth certificate, driver's license, as well as her mother's death certificate, to obtain the family history she longed for. It seemed to take forever to obtain it. Finally, she received a letter dated October 10, 1983, with the information and answers she was looking for! She kindly shares that information so that we can all learn about the Orphan Train exactly as it was—no rose-colored glasses! For this we gratefully thank Kathleen!

Catherine respectfully called her father "Papa." Other children her age made fun of the Orphan Train children. Her father explained being an orphan quite simply. He told Catherine, "Most babies just come; we asked for a dark-haired baby girl, and that's exactly what we got!"

Catherine's lifelong best friend was left on the doorstep of an Irish neighborhood. She was named Annie. She looked to be three weeks old. Catherine and Annie rode the same train to West Point, Nebraska, on December 13, 1912. They were two of a total of 19 children on the train. The *West Point Republican* newspaper read: "They were delivered to the persons who had previously pledged themselves to take them. The sweet little tots were passed into waiting arms. These little ones will have good homes and will be cared for with love as boundless as the prairies to which they have come."

Catherine's elderly parents were very religious. Catherine and her girlfriend Annie really enjoyed going to the Church with them to decorate the Church altar. It is interesting to note both friends named one of their daughters "Kathleen"!

Catherine's name was sometimes spelled with a "C" and sometimes spelled with a "K." Her birth certificate shows a "C." Her indenture papers show a "K."

Catherine's father was a carpenter and a woodcarver. Sadly, the church in which he had carved the statuary, cabinets and altars burned down, destroying many thousands of dollars' worth of irreplaceable work.

Catherine was baptized at the Holy Cross Catholic Church in Brooklyn, New York. She was buried at the Holy Cross Catholic Church in Beemer, Nebraska.

In kitchens, we often see "Lazy Susans" in cupboards. For a short period of time during the days of the Foundling Hospital, there was a "Lazy Susan" type of structure in the door to receive babies, thus taking them out of the elements!

An additional note shared by Mary Ellen Johnson, Founder of the Orphan Train Heritage Society of America, Inc.:

Mary Ellen gives us a clearer picture of how the New York Foundling Hospital received babies. It was through a passage consisting of a basket into which the baby could be placed. The door could be turned, thus taking the baby out of the elements. It was a "Lazy Susan" type of structure, and it was only used for a short time. Sister Irene used a rather novel approach to help keep the little ones alive. She posted a notice at the basket to immediately inform her when a baby was being placed. This gave her an opportunity to invite the mother (if she was the person placing the baby) to come in and not only nurse her own baby but to nurse at least one other. Often a mother became so attached to her child that she sought the means to keep the baby.

Catherine and Annie

Catherine with her indentured parents, Ferdinand and Mary Anna

Catherine

CHARLOTTE M. ENDORF

Long awaited letter from the
New York
Foundling Hospital!

The New York | Center for Parent
Foundling Hospital | and Child Development

1175 THIRD AVENUE, NEW YORK, N.Y. 10021 / TEL: (212) 472-2233

October 10, 1983

Ms. Kathleen Downy
907 Avenue E
Wisner, Nebraska 68791

Dear Ms. Downy:

Your mother's biological name was Katherine Hackett. After the
Indenture and adoption she was known as Catherine Walter.

Catherine Walter's biological mother was Katherine Murray who was
born in Canada. She was forty-four years old when her daughter
was born.

Catherine's biological father was William Hackett who was born in the
U.S.A. He was a carpenter and was forty-three years old when his
daughter was born.

Catherine was the 5th child. As you know she was born in St. Mary's
Hospital in Brooklyn, New York on November 14, 1910. She was baptized
at St. Mary's Hospital on November 22, 1910 by Rev. John Woods. She
was placed in the New York Foundling Hospital on December 15, 1910
by her mother who surrendered her for Indenture or adoption. Her
mother gave us no further information except that she was unable
to care for Katherine.

On October 13, 1912 Catherine was adopted by Ferdinand and Marie
Walter of West Point, Nebraska. She acquired six "adopted" brothers
and one "adopted" sister.

Her "adopted" mother, Marie, died in 1919 and her "adopted" father
died in 1926. Catherine continued to live with her sister and brothers.

I thought perhaps you might like to have a copy of Catherine's
Record of Birth and copies of her letters in her own handwriting.

I have given you everything that is in her record and hope that
it will help to fill in the "empty spaces."

May the dear Lord bless you, your brothers, sisters, children
and nieces and nephews!

Sincerely yours,

Sister Marian Healy, S.C.
Sister Marian Healy, S.C.
Supervisor, Record Information

SMH/aj

Enc.

74

This Indenture, made this *13* day of *January*
in the year of our Lord One Thousand Nine Hundred and *thirteen* between
THE NEW YORK FOUNDLING HOSPITAL, a Corporation incorporated and organized under the Laws
of the State of New York, party of the first part, and *Ferdinand Traller*
and *Marya* , his wife, of *West Point*
State of *Neb.* , part *is* of the second part:

WHEREAS, *Katherine Hackett* female child,
now of the age of *four* years and *one* months,
was heretofore, pursuant to the provisions of the Charter of the aforesaid Corporation, received and
taken, and now is under its care and custody, and has now, in the judgement of its Board of Managers,
arrived at a suitable age for the said Corporation to indenture.

Now, THEREFORE, this Indenture WITNESSETH, that the said party of the first part, in and by
virtue of the power and authority conferred upon and possessed by it, under and by chapter three
hundred and nineteen of the Laws of the State of New York for the year 1848, chapter six hundred
and thirty-five of the Laws of said State for the year 1872, and chapter nineteen of the Laws of said
State for the year 1909, being chapter fourteen of the Consolidated Laws known as the Domestic
Relations Law, do hereby put, place and indenture the said *Katherine Hackett*
unto the said part *is* of the second part, as *their* own child in every respect until
the said *Katherine Hackett* shall arrive at the age of Eighteen years,
to live with, and be employed by the said part *is* of the second part in and about *their*
house and household, and the affairs thereof, and to be instructed therein, and also as hereinafter
specified, during all of which time the said female child shall reside with and obey said part *is*
of the second part, and according to her power, will and ability shall honestly orderly and obediently
in all things demean and behave herself toward the part *is* of the second part.

The part *is* of the second part agree *s* as follows:

I.—That during all the time aforesaid *Ferd. and Marya Traller* will
provide said *Katherine Hackett* with suitable and proper board, lodging
and medical attendance, and all things necessary and fit for any indentured child, and in all respects
similar to what would ordinarily be provided and allowed by the said part *is* of the second part,
or one in *their* station of life, for *their* own child or children.

If the said child is returned to the party of the first part when she shall reach the age of Eighteen
years, then the part *is* of the second part will give to said child a new Bible, a complete
suit of new clothes, together with all those she shall then have in use, and an outfit of at least
the same in every respect as their own child.

II.—That the said part *is* of the second part will teach and instruct, or cause to be taught
or instructed, said child in all branches of education ordinarily taught to the children of persons in the
station of life of the said part *is* of the second part, such being the ordinary branches of school
education and such as are required by law, including reading, writing and the general rules of arith-
metic, and will bring her up in a moral and correct manner, and in the Catholic faith, and cause and
procure said child to behave herself in all things as all minor children should demean themselves,
during their minority and generally that said child shall be maintained, clothed, educated and treated
with like care and tenderness as if she were in fact the child of the part *is* of the second part
and will provide for said child, financially and in every other way, as if the said child were adopted
by the said part *is* of the second part under the laws of the State of New York.

III.—That the said part *is* of the second part will not, nor will *their* legal
representatives or assigns, assign or transfer this Indenture to any other person without the consent
in writing of the party of the first part.

Page 1 of Indenture Paperwork

Catherine

Catherine

Catherine and Joe on their wedding day!

Catherine participating in parade at Beemer, Nebraska.

Catherine and Joe

Children of Joe and Catherine: (Left to Right – Back Row) Lambert (L.W.), Clarence, LeRoy; (Left to Right – Front Row) JoAnn, Debra, Kathleen.

77

CHAPTER 12

Harold — Deceased rider from Ainsworth, Nebraska. Author talked by phone with son of Gordon, Nebraska. Brother of Ed, George, Jack (John), and Robert.

Ed — Deceased rider from Los Angeles, California. Author talked by phone with nephews in Gordon, Nebraska, and Vacaville, California. Brother of Harold, George, Jack (John), and Robert.

George — Deceased rider from Fremont, Nebraska. Author talked by phone with nephews in Gordon, Nebraska, and Vacaville, California. Brother of Harold, Ed, Jack (John), and Robert.

Jack (John) — Deceased rider from Omaha, Nebraska. Author talked by phone with son in Omaha, Nebraska; daughter in Niwot, Colorado; and nephews in Gordon, Nebraska, and Vacaville, California. Brother of Harold, Ed, George, and Robert.

Robert A. — Deceased rider from San Diego, California. Author talked by phone with nephew in Gordon, Nebraska, and son in Vacaville, California. Brother of Harold, Ed, George, and Jack (John).

Personal Interview with Harold's Son James:

Five brothers took a ride aboard the Orphan Train the Fall of 1922. Harold was thirteen years old at the time. Their stories are much the same as the rest. Their train ride started in New York, where their father had died and their mother could not care for them. They were placed with the Children's Aid Society and put on the Orphan Train. Although for many years the brothers did not talk much about being orphans, they told the world when they were featured on a television news segment April 2, 1989.

Once off the train, the boys were separated and sent to different homes in Nebraska; however, they were allowed to keep in touch. All but Ed felt they were placed in good homes with kind and loving families. Ed felt his foster parents only wanted cheap labor and a farmhand. He vividly recalled a severe beating he had once endured.

Harold described his rural upbringing on a farm near Tekamah, Nebraska, as very fine, with foster parents who were religious people. He felt very close to them.

Their stories show that, if you work hard, you can be anything you desire! All of the brothers helped each other become successful. They were determined to overcome any obstacle set in their way. Even though Harold was next to the bottom of his class his first year of high school, it was then that he decided he better start making something of his life, and he was old enough to do so. He set his mind to study, and studied real hard for the next three years, and graduated as salutatorian of his Class of 1928.

After high school graduation, Harold attended Des Moines University in Des Moines, Iowa, for one year. James tells tales of how his dad raised bees and sold honey. Harold had 50 swarms of bees of his own and worked as a beekeeper in Tekamah to earn money to return to college. Harold then attended Nebraska Wesleyan University and graduated in 1933 with a Bachelor of Arts degree. He promptly started working on his Master of Arts degree in physiology and anatomy, and received that degree on June 4, 1937. At the same time, he was attending the University of Nebraska School of Medicine at Omaha and received his Doctor of Medicine degree on June 7, 1937. He remained in Omaha, and had a rotating internship at the Methodist Hospital. After completing his internship, Harold served in the Armed Forces for a year.

On February 1, 1939, Harold moved to Bassett, Nebraska, to practice medicine. He opened a two-room office in the basement of the old Buckendorf building (which now houses the *Rock County Leader* newspaper). In 1940, Harold built his own hospital in Bassett. He ran that for 21 years until the Rock County Hospital was built in 1961. In 1971, he moved his practice to Ainsworth, Nebraska. He retired in 1987 after completing 50 years of service in the medical field. A water fountain with a plaque was erected in his honor at the Fairgrounds in Bassett, Nebraska, for his many years of dedication to the Sandhills area.

His brother Ed also became a doctor. He practiced in California. George was a regional manager of an insurance company at Fremont, Nebraska. Jack (John) worked with Harold for years in Bassett, Nebraska. He later was an employee of Nebraska Methodist Hospital in Omaha, Nebraska. In September of 1969 he became Credit Manager there. Robert was a Methodist minister in California.

At age 80, Harold was married to JoAnn. His brother Robert officiated at the wedding. One of Harold's favorite pastimes was fishing with family members. Harold passed away in 1992. His four brothers have also passed away. They leave behind many Orphan Train descendants who have followed in their ancestors' footsteps with successful medical and professional careers.

John has passed away; however, on his 68th birthday he wrote his autobiography that his daughter Ruth has kindly shared with us! Learn more about the era from John in his own words:

"Autobiography"

~ John

"On October 20, 1922, my four brothers—Edward, 16; Harold, 13; Robert, 10; George, 4; and myself, 7—were charged to Agnes (Alice) Bogardus, who boarded an 'Orphan Train' with us and traveled to Tekamah, Nebraska. We were lined up on the stage in the Lyric Theater and Miss Bogardus expounded a short synopsis about each one of us. Immediately henceforth the people from the audience came on stage and asked questions about all of us until each one of us was chosen. We all began our new and beautiful homes.

"My parents, Leo and Lillian, spent many years and a wonderful amount of time and energy raising me on the farm. I graduated from Jackson High School in 1934.

"I attended Nebraska Wesleyan University off and on from 1934 to 1941 as a pre-medical student, preaching part time with an exhorter's license to help defray expenses.

"During this time I lived with a professor at Nebraska Wesleyan University and her family until I entered the Army 2/20/41.

"I became a pharmacist in the U.S. Army Medical Corps and was honorably discharged as First Sergeant of the 201st Station Hospital at Cold Bay, Alaska, 9/25/45.

"Kathryn, my lovely lady, and I were united in marriage 7/28/46. We were blessed with 4 beautiful children plus a bonus of an extra twin.

"Through the years I entered the fields of selling vacuum cleaners, disposals, women's apparel, Watkins products, groceries, real estate, insurance, and honey by the pound door to door. I was a football official for 5 years and drove a taxi for 2 days only. I owned a service station for 2 years.

"I entered the apiary business with 1,250 colonies of bees that produced 140,000 pounds of honey one year. I injured my back seriously and a spinal fusion was performed in 1958. We bought a grocery store and built a trailer court around it in Chico, California. I bought a hospital in 1950. Kathryn lived with cancer for 7 years until 1977. I am Past Master of Bassett Lodge #254.

"I retired as Credit Manager of Nebraska Methodist Hospital in Omaha, Nebraska, 9/26/79, after which I visited the friendly and most interesting Hawaiian Islands, Denmark, Germany, Egypt, and the historical and most fabulous Holy Lands."

John's minister at the church that John and his wife Kathryn attended wrote a wonderful 14-page biography dated March 14, 1991, about John and his brothers. John's children Leo and Ruth are delighted to share a segment of the biography with you that focuses on his early life to enrich yet further the Orphan Train story.

"The Orphan Train"
By: Rev. J. Kenneth Kimberlin
Omaha, Nebraska

"John was born on September 26, 1915, in Freeport, Long Island, to Herman and Martha. He remembers that his father took very sick one day and died of double pneumonia. John recalls seeing his father in the casket. Shortly after his father's death, John's mother was confined to an institution where she died in 1953. The five brothers had nowhere to go but to an orphanage; the year was 1917. Five years later, they were all transferred on the 'Orphan Train' to Tekamah, Nebraska.
More than 150,000 of these orphans had been relocated throughout the Midwest and South this way since 1854.

"The 'Orphan Train' system was conceived by Charles Loring Brace, founder of the Children's Aid Society of New York. Brace wrote that 'The best of all asylums for the outcast child is the farmer's home.' This proved to be true in many cases where families were eager to take them in, raise them as one of their own, and provide 'extra hands' for the farm. Many more children were treated as nothing more than 'slaves.'

"John remembers when his older brother Ed, then 16, took John from first grade school and the Smith Orphanage in New York City, to board the bus. John remembers crying as he left. Before that time, John remembers only the cut finger which still shows a scar, and the apples given him at a big parade when he was around 3 years old. It was Armistice Day at the close of World War One, November 11, 1916.

"When they arrived in Tekamah, Nebraska, their chaperone on the long train ride, Alice Bogardus, had them line up on the stage of the Lyric Theater and told a story about each orphan. People would come up on stage, look the line of orphans over, ask questions, and choose one or more to go home with them. Leo and Lillian chose John, age 7, and his youngest brother, George, who was 4 years old. They took them home and raised them as their own children.

"Lillian was 22 years old at the time. She and Leo raised the two boys to be good Christians. 'Mom' said many times, 'If you can't say anything good about someone, just don't say anything at all.' Their

'Mother' had projects going for them all the time to keep them busy. She was a good church worker, and had hundreds of friends all over the world.

"In fact, she was in Innsbruck, Austria, when she died of a heart attack in 1979 at the age of 79. Her husband Leo preceded her in death in 1975 at the age of 84.

"John remembers most of the many pets he had while a boy growing up on that Nebraska farm. He had two dogs, Bim Gump, a terrier, and Ry, a German Shepherd police dog; 3 ducks, 6 chickens, and took care of one calf, 2 cows, 2 horses and 500 pigs. He participated in 4-H, Boy Scouts, and gardening during his 19 years on that farm.

"From October of 1922 to May of 1929, John attended the Fairview Grade School. Then he went to Riverside High School near Tekamah, Nebraska, for three years. His senior year was spent at Jackson High School near Lincoln, Nebraska. Those were great years, except for a broken right arm cranking a tractor in 1930, and a severe back injury lifting a very large and heavy block of cement in 1931. In spite of these mishaps, John was chosen cheerleader with twins, Ruth and Beth. He also lettered in track and sang in the choir. Through his Boy Scout troop, he helped build a Scout building in 1933, but hurt his back again in the process. When he graduated from High School in 1934, he vowed with his classmates to have a reunion annually. He has kept his vow for 57 years.

"After graduation, John managed tearing down a very large house, helped build the Bassett hospital, worked on a farm part time, went to Nebraska Wesleyan University part time, and even preached six months at La Salle Methodist Church in Beatrice, Nebraska, with an exhorter's license. He also sang in *The Mikado* and *Pirates of Penzance*."

Personal Interview with Robert A.'s Son Robert M.:

Robert A. was born in 1913. He was about nine when he came on the Orphan Train to Nebraska from New York. He graduated from Nebraska Wesleyan University and became a pastor at the First Methodist Church in Sacramento, California. He married Jean. They had two children. He enjoyed traveling and led many tours throughout the world from the 1950s to the 1980s. His brothers John and George's foster mother, Lillian, was on a tour he was guiding in Austria in 1979 when she had a heart attack and passed away.

Robert M. kindly shares with us a slightly edited version of his dad's story about Grand Central Station. Robert A. included it in his sermon on "The Christian Connection" in San Diego, California, on August 30, 1987. His dad was 75 years old at the time. Robert M. truly treasures the tape recording:

"Everybody really needs somebody, and sometimes just anybody will do. A long time ago, when I was a little boy about 7, I was at Grand Central Station in New York City, alone, trying to sell newspapers. I didn't know it was illegal to do that. I spotted a 'whitecap'—a kind of Grand Central Station policeman—coming toward me; and the vicious frown on his face told me I was in big trouble. Frightened, I headed down the subway steps. But on the very first landing, guess what? TWO whitecaps were coming up the steps! I panicked. I froze right on the spot. It was hopeless, I thought.

"But just about then, a tall man—and it was winter and he was wearing a long coat—was coming up the steps. He sized up the situation and looked into my wide-eyed, fright-filled eyes. He quickened his pace, reached me, opened his coat, closed it with me inside and walked briskly to the nearest exit. Then I shot out of the coat, cheering my new-won freedom as I raced down the street. My cheer was genuine.

"Everybody needs somebody. All my life I have needed somebody—teachers, Sunday School, farmer families, ministers, congregations, personal friends, marriage, critics, encouragers—all have me in common. I needed them. These were caring connections with me. And everyone ought to be able to write his own autobiography with such connections."

Robert A. passed away in 1995 and is buried in San Diego, California.

Edward, the oldest of the brothers, was born in 1907. He became a doctor. He served in Okinawa during World War II. He passed away in Los Angeles, California, in 1991.

Robert A. in New York, age 9

ORPHAN CHILDREN HERE FRIDAY

ELEVEN BOYS AND GIRLS FROM

Newspaper headline from the Burt County Herald, *October, 26, 1922. (Harold, Ed, George, John, and Robert came on this Orphan Train from New York.)*

The brothers posed for a photo in Nebraska.

Robert A. receives an honorary Doctor of Divinity degree from Nebraska Wesleyan University in 1952.

George in New York, age 3

John in New York, age 5

Harold in New York, age 12

John – January 1942

George and John

Leo and Lillian – Photo taken during the early years of their marriage, possibly about the time they took in John and George.

Ed was serving in Okinawa during World War II when this photo was taken.

Harold, September 26, 1989, with 18 lb. 3 oz., 42-inch Northern Pike!

87

AFTERWORD

Although an Orphan Train rider or descendant may have directly affected us, perhaps we have been unaware. As an author and a Nebraska resident, I have always lived close to the railroad. I sometimes wonder how many orphans I have encountered in my life without even knowing it. Could this be true for you as well?

This book was written so that this very important segment of American History would not be lost. In 1991, 22 actual riders attended the 30th Annual Orphan Train Celebration in Auburn, Nebraska. Nebraskans provided homes to 3,442 youths between 1854 and 1910, according to the 1910 Annual Report of the New York Children's Aid Society. I attended the 2005 Nebraska Orphan Train Annual Celebration this year in Broken Bow, Nebraska, where there were, sadly, only two original riders present. At the time of this publishing, one of those two has passed away. Each June there is also a national gathering for riders, descendants, and interested parties at the National Headquarters in Concordia, Kansas. I attended in 2005 to find five actual riders present.

Time has crept up on the original Orphan Train riders so, as an author, I have traveled the many necessary miles to seek them out so as to preserve their precious stories. The purpose of this book is to bring to life this part of American History which many had no idea existed before my project began. It excites me that we can keep this history alive!

ABOUT THE ILLUSTRATOR

Sarah M. Endorf has been living with borreliosis since March of 2004. She knows that as with any adversity she needs to focus on the positive. Although she is only sixteen years old, she and her mother, Charlotte, published a book *After the Rain, Oh the Beautiful Rainbow* in July of 2005. It is an inspirational and heroic true story about her battle with the disease. *After the Rain* provides thoughtful insights, encouragement, and support to anyone facing adversity.

After the Rain provides practical guidance and information about the results and remedies of this increasingly common disease in easy-to-understand terms, as seen through the eyes of one of its intended victims who is day by day escaping its grasp.

Sarah has continued to excel, and has shown her God-given talent by illustrating this book *Plains Bound: Fragile Cargo* by her mother, Charlotte. Although Sarah continues to suffer severe arthritic-type joint pain, she was insistent and persistent in doing a little bit daily toward her goal of completing the project by the deadline. Some days that little bit meant just planning for what would be done on her next "good" day when her hands would cooperate! Thankfully, her hands did cooperate, and her illustrations are absolutely beautiful!

Orphan Train riders and their descendants became Sarah's dear friends as this book progressed. On turning 16, she received birthday greetings from many of them. She shares a special poem that one Orphan Train rider sent to her:

SARAH
Written by: Lester
November 1, 2005

You rise up every morning
To face the light of day,
You never know what will happen
Or what may come your way

You have to play the hand you get
As you go along life's path
And hope we have a winning hand
To last us through the day

Happy Birthday Darling
Although we've never met,
For I know that by the Grace of God
You'll win the battle yet.

ABOUT THE AUTHOR

Charlotte M. Endorf uses the technology of today to work flexible hours out of her own home. In July of 2005 she and her 15-year-old daughter, Sarah, authored a motivational/inspirational book entitled *After the Rain, Oh the Beautiful Rainbow!* She inspires and educates audiences with her professional talks designed to complement each book. She has her own Internet-based business in which she links individuals with Fortune 500 companies, teaching them how to profit from the Internet. Utilizing "exclusive" products from her online business, she has opened a spa out of her own home in which she treats individuals to the wonderfully relaxing, invigorating, and inspiring experience of her Spa Café. The spa is also mobile for those who prefer the comfort of their own home. She works out of her home and on demand as a Travel Representative/ Tour Guide.

She has been a member of Toastmasters International for over a decade. She has worked her way to the top coveted award of "Distinguished Toastmaster." She has given dozens of speeches at her club, to civic groups, and has participated in many speech competitions. She is currently working her way to the "top" a second time. Only a handful of people in the organization have reached this goal. In 2003, she earned the award of "Toastmaster of the Decade" for the District. Because of popularity and demand, after only five months on the Humanities Council Speakers Bureau, she was named to their "high-use" list! Those on the "high-use" list constitute speakers who conduct at least 3% of the total amount of Speakers Bureau programs in a calendar year!

She has a love for children. She marvels at watching their eyes light up as they discover how exciting American History lessons can be by listening to her talks. Her dream was to become a professional speaker and to author books! Her daughter Sarah, much to her delight, follows in those same footsteps!

"Save a space for rainbows and dreams."
          – Author Unknown

9 781598 002355